4 ft 8 1/2
By
CW Mills
AND ALL THAT
FOR MANIACS ONLY

Ian Allan
PUBLISHING

IN FAIRNESS TO EVERYONE
ELSE THE AUTHOR-ARTIST OF
THIS MONOGRAPH
W. MILLS
WISHES TO DEDICATE IT TO HIMSELF

First published 2007

ISBN (10) 0 7110 0061 1
ISBN (13) 978 0 7110 0061 2

Published by Ian Allan Publishing

an imprint of Ian Allan Publishing Ltd, Hersham, Surrey KT12 4RG.
Printed in England by Ian Allan Printing Ltd, Hersham, Surrey KT12 4RG.

Code: 0710/A1

Visit the Ian Allan Publishing website at www.ianallanpublishing.com

BEFORE I FORGET,

or a sort of Introduction

For many years it has been dawning upon me that there is a rich mine of true national character lying under the foundations of those dear, almost extinct, yet never forgotten, railways of ours; and before all traces are blotted out, and the willow herb takes over the tracks, I feel that it is only right and proper that one who understands, and feels deeply for them, should take up his pen and record for posterity their history and charm.

What is the Englishman able to do which lesser breeds find impossible, apart from watching cricket matches? Why, of course, he can laugh at himself! though I must warn anyone outside the pale that it is not permitted for *him* to laugh at *us!*

Well now, RAILWAYS. Those pieces of steel which snake over this green island in ordered parallels, and only occasionally go mad and get knotted up at places like Clapham. They are our national nerves, and if you have nerves, you must expect headaches!

I have called in a number of experts to set down their memories of railways from alpha to omega and although an occasional smile may creep in, I beg of you not to mock them; for there is no more tender, sensitive, animal than the true railway maniac, and I know you wouldn't want to hurt his feelings.

One day a man thought of a number . . .

IN THE BEGINNING

ONE day a man thought of a number – 485. He toyed about with it and got 4.85. He still didn't think it was quite right, so he made it 4 feet 8.5 inches. That was it! He jumped out of his bath and ran (or was that somebody else?) then, still uncertain, he tried 4 feet $8\frac{3}{4}$ inches and plain 4 feet, but quickly saw that they were nowhere near as good.

There was another fellow about then who thought of 7 feet, but he was an eccentric anyhow. Well, his name shows you that – Isambard Kingdom. If there is anyone here who is a G.W. fan, I must add that I am not taking sides; I am just recording the facts, but think what 7 feet would have meant with land values as they are now!

To return to the better figure – 4 feet and a bit, you know of course that this was the distance between the wheels of Roman chariots, so you see, Ben Hur was, in a sense, one of the fathers of railways.

There was another man who could be called a pioneer and his name was Hero, I think; he invented a sort of steam turbine engine but he hadn't any lines for it to run

---

The illustration above shews Brunton's Mechanical Traveller being tried out on the Lickey Incline with spiked boots on.

on so he decided to wait until James Watt was born. Watt! There's a name of great import, he was a great inventor, not only of electric kettles, but of a lot of very funny music hall jokes too. He really did find the power behind pressurised steam, and once that was found, it was only a matter of time before places like Stockton and Darlington were campaigning for railway lines to run things on. About that time, Robert Louis Stephenson had just been travelling on a donkey in France and thought how much nicer it would have been to travel on a train and being another inventive man (he invented Treasure Island, remember) *he decided to put wheels on the kettle James Watt had left boiling* and to run it between Stockton and Darlington.

It was not long before engines were being built by famous companies such as Stephenson Bros, Trevithic and Camel, Boulton and Watt, What and Whosits, and Bolton and Wanderers – all now leading members of the Locomotive Manufacturers Association.

Well that's about it for a start.

4′ 8½″ was the distance between Roman chariot wheels.

Mineral traffic was mostly carried on the early lines but soon they took brass bands, church choirs, cows, flag days, men in funny hats, and barrels of beer on the tenders.

These days-out were not taken as lightly as might at first appear. Have you noticed what they called them? *Trips?* No, *Jaunts?* No, EXCURSIONS – There's a real name for you. Can you honestly say that you ever hear that word and don't connect it up with railway travel? Of course not, whenever I hear it I can almost smell the steam and hot oil as the *Cauliflower* simmers at the front and then lets out a shrill shriek; slips and roars as the six-wheelers edge forward with the Blackpool bound Whit-weekenders.

By the way, if you are puzzled by the idea of having a vegetable on the front of a train, then this book is not for you. You are not one of us. I'm sorry, but that's one of the test questions for entry into the railway maniacs' circle. Still, if you really want to go on, you can, but don't blame me if you are puzzled by other cryptic references such as jumbos or potato cans, but you really will come across a lot of things you won't be able to understand if you are not one of the initiated.

Picture an early excursion from say Stockton to Darlington – they hadn't invented Blackpool or anywhere else for

Some lords of the manor
took their coaches on a flat wagon.

that matter yet! Flags waving, bands playing, engine coughing along – and talking of coughing, pneumonia was a matter of course for all third-class travellers in those days. The coach, ha! COACH! was a mere box on wheels with a hole in the floor for the rain to run out. Some lords of the manor took their own coaches on a flat waggon and most unsafe did they look, if you ask me!

However, after W. S. Gilbert had drawn attention to the rude scribblings on window panes, they brought in an Act of Parliament to make all railways promise to carry third class passengers in closed cattle waggons; the shareholders didn't like it a bit, nor did the cattle, in fact I suspect that this was the beginning of the rift which grew up between the railways and cows. Oh yes, it's there all right. Have you ever noticed how *cows deliberately snub a passing train?* They are sometimes quite vulgar about it. It's not good enough when you think how the early railway people gave them rides around Gloucester and Bath. Still that's gratitude I suppose.

Well now let's forget the unpleasantness and sum up. The railways grew and waxed great. There was the – Greenwich to – er where did it go to ? and the Canterbury to ? and the Inner Circle, the Outer Circle, the Spiral, the Great Tangent, and the Q.E.D. all booming along with a board of directors made up of G. Hudson.

Oh yes, do you recall I.K. from a few pages back ? Well we must mention his Atmospheric Pollution Railway. How did it work ? Well, not very well, but the idea was sound enough, the engines stood still and sucked instead of puffing and the carriages were in a tube which was air-tight, in theory. Clear ? well I did warn you that some things were very technical to the novice.

I tell you what, let's go on to the next chapter, it's about engines, so now for some real information.

Cow, deliberately snubbing passing train.

An Early Works Visit

AARONS or Ahrons was one of the first locomotive addicts, but that's taking things a little too far back so we will start after that.

Since wet steam first oozed into a cylinder and pushed a piston back there have been many and varied ideas to improve on this. Much midnight wick has been expended at places like Crewe, Derby, Horwich, Brighton, Swindon and all stations to Evercreech, by such giants as Webb, Aspinall, Ramsbottom, Stirling, Moss, and many another in their attempts to make these improvements. Thus by their unstinted efforts we now have wet steam oozing into a cylinder and pushing a piston back. Anyhow, design has improved. Look at funnels. In the early days they had great long things, whereas now they are speedy looking and they put smoke blinkers on to take the smoke out of the driver's eyes. And take the cabs, all mod. cons., h. and c. solid fuel heating, bell system, the lot!

Now we are wandering from the point. I sometimes do that. Oh yes, the Development of the early locomotive to its present advanced state. Well, when wet steam first – oh dear. Suppose you have a look at the drawings opposite for a bit while I read what I've said up to now.

You will have noticed from the foregoing diagrams, if the printers have made them forego that is, that the number of wheels soon started to grow on the early locomotives. This is a very interesting point, and one I am determined to clear up – braking power, that's what they were for. It is well understood that friction is the crux of the matter, and only right too. Well, the more wheels, the more braking surface. It's as simple as that. Oh I know that some other railway know-alls will dispute this, they will tell you that you are a fool to waste good money on a book by a maniac like me. Worry not my friend; they do no service to the noble pursuit of railway mania.

Back to wheels, I will admit one other reason for this multiplication of the number of wheels. The designers liked to see plenty about and I can understand them, I like a nice selection of drivers and ponies myself.

This matter of brakes is very serious you know. The early engineers never had any trouble with horses and they expected to go on merrily with iron horses. They little knew. You should have tried to stop *Ajax* when in full cry, or *Locomotion* when it was really locomoting. The poor drivers used to throw the whole thing into reverse. What was the result? – Tank engines!

From wheels the natural sequitur is 'Wheel Arrangements'. 2-2-0 soon became 2-2-2 and soon 2-4-0 then 4-4-0, and so on to 4-6-0, 2-8-0, 2-10-0, even 2-2-2-2, bet that's got you puzzled! Think now – *Greater Britain* – Yes, Webb was certainly a teazer for wheels! He liked 'em separate too, none of your coupling rods. The Americans liked wheels too and though perhaps it's cheating, I feel the Americans don't count; they have more than one dome and everything (including the kitchen sink) hanging all over them, so we had better leave them out, I'm sure they won't mind, for they have their cow catchers too. I often wish we could catch a cow on an engine just to teach it not to be so rude, I wouldn't want to hurt it of course, but then can you imagine a dear little 0-6-0 hurting anybody; they are too good natured!

Result of too enthusiastic use of brakes?

I expect the G.W.R. fans are champing at the bit and asking 'When is he going to talk about a *real* railway?' All right, I will now introduce you to the greatest, west-ernest gentleman that ever built a bridge at Saltash or managed to launch a ship that was too big to be of any real use, but by jingo, what a ship!

Isambard Kingdom Brunel, or as his close friends used to call him, Isambard Kingdom Brunel, was not, repeat NOT a locomotive designer. You may be surprised to learn this unless you are a G.W. fan (one or two people are not, strange to say). However Brunel – we will risk it and miss off the Isambard Kingdom – did design almost everything else; he designed a surgical instrument for getting coins out of the throats of silly people who will suck things; he designed a tunnel boring shield (or was that his father? – anyway it is in the family); he also designed the Great Western Railway and the *Great Eastern* – no not the railway, but the ship.

'To the Directors of the Great Western Railway. Sirs, As from Sunday next you will kindly run all trains on a track with metals 4′ 8½″ apart. Hoping this finds you, etc., etc.'

His ambition was to build bigger and better than ever before, and he jolly well achieved it!

I suspect he had a hand in the design of that loco called *Ajax* which had plate driving wheels of huge size. Note the adjective, HUGE, that smacks of Brunel to me. *Ajax* was not a success and had difficulty in moving herself and though she might have failed (unless you're a G.W. fan), THE GREAT WESTERN certainly did not fail. It soon had all the other railways wishing that they had built seven-foot tracks, and in a way this was to be the undoing of the G.W. because the other railways ganged up on it later and bullied it shockin' until it had to conform to the right and proper gauge.

I do not remember the broad gauge myself, but perhaps you do, after all I'm only a slip of a thing, but who could forget *Lord of the Isles*? That great driving wheel without a flange too. Yes, Brunel had invented a thing called 'magnetic adhesion' to keep it on the rails; he was certainly well ahead of his time and I often dream of a meeting between him and a certain Doctor B, and I drop off the heavy suppers for a while afterwards.

I could write a whole book about Brunel, but I'm not much of a typist and this is giving me arm ache anyway, but why not ask your local librarian if he has a book about great railway engineers. He will lead you gently away by the arm and all the other people who heard will raise their eyebrows and think how sad for a grown man like you to want to read about 'puffers'. Pay no attention, let them go on looking for Lolita, you are one of the elect and can afford to be silent.

Well, back now to this seven-foot gauge. They had a lot of trouble with it – metal fatigue, you know. They didn't understand anything about it then, and if they heard a piece of metal track yawning they put it down to the sleepers – or the fact that the carriage wheels were tyred. Just as I must have my little joke so had they their's on the G.W. in the shape of a very humorous engine called *Hurricane*. This was an engine in two, no *three*

The Crampton type of locomotive was popular in France.

'Voici Le Crampton. Il est dans le jardin de ma tante.'

'Hurricane' at speed.

parts! Starting from the back, TENDER, BOILER, and in front the driving parts WITH GEARS! It was quite a sight and quite a sound, when the driver changed down. Talk about double de-clutching, the gearing made 6 ft drivers equivalent to 18 ft. wheels!

This idea of getting bigger and better wheels had a big drawback and I'm afraid I shall have to be rather scientific here.

SCIENTIFIC BIT: Wheels are (usually) circles, the bigger the circle the higher the centre or hub; the higher the hub the more it gets in the way of the boiler, so if you must have big wheels –

1. Sling 'em above the boiler – *see Cornwall.*
2. Put wheel behind boiler – *see* Mr. Crampton.

Mr. Trevithick trying to remember where he put that boiler!

3. Put wheels on a different truck – *Hurricane.*
4. Push axle through boiler.

NOTE. Somebody *did* try No. 4, but no trace of his notes, made after the event have been found – nor was he.

END OF SCIENTIFIC BIT.

There is one other interesting fact about early engines – they didn't smoke. I can see you do by your fingers. It's a silly habit you know and they wouldn't let engines out at first unless they promised not to smoke. Well, there were no washing powders in those days or I.T.V. to support them, so think of the mess it could make on the clothes by the line. In fact they were so strict about this smoking business that some poor engines actually had to consume their own smoke.

THE argument and confusion as to which was the best way of making a steam engine, got to such a pitch in 1829 A.D. that the great Liverpool and Manchester railway said they couldn't stand it any longer and they would hold a grand competition.

The rules were strict:

1. The engine with carriages, shall run *by hand* to the starting point.
2. As soon as steam is got to 50 lb per sq. in. (for measuring which the designer is to provide a working gauge), the engine shall set off on its test journey.
3. The Editor's decision is final.

I will give you the runners and riders:

1. *Novelty* (Braithwait & Ericsson).
2. *Sanspareil* (T. Hackworth).
3. *Perseverance* (Burstall & Hill).
4. *Cyclometer*, or *Centipede?* (Brandreth).
5. *Rocket* (Stephenson).

Sanspareil looked so much like *Rocket* that the judges called for a photo, but as they hadn't been invented yet they disqualified it.

Novelty was a sort of tank engine and was disqualified because it didn't look right.

SIX
FIVE
FOUR
THREE
TWO
ONE
ROCKET
ZERO

Cyclopede or Centimetre, was horse-powered. Yes, a real horse and I'm afraid she was disqualified. I suspect doping, but it was hushed up.

Perseverance persevered like mad, but as was usually the case, disqualification took place in accordance with the rules and that left *ROCKET* the winner.

Stephenson showed just how well *Rocket* could go in a demonstration run by doing 23 miles without disqualification taking place.

Picture the scene: All systems 'GO': 10-9-8-7-6-5-4-3-2-1, ZERO. Blast off. Oh, I should have liked to have been there and to have seen the little engine belting through Chat Moss – yes through it because as yet they hadn't found a way to go on top of it. *Cyclopede's* horse took fright and raced off to Aintree to do the first Grand National. That's how it was founded, you know.

But seriously though, have you ever thought how very different it all might have been if *Cyclelamp* had won? Think of the number of horses you would have needed

Old print of Olive Mount Cutting showing artist at work. It is probable that this is J. M. W. Turner at work on his well-known picture called 'Rain, Rain and Rain.'

inside the engines to do the run from Euston to Glasgow, for it was actually expected that *Cyclopede* was going to win, because the L.N.W.R. put down special water troughs in readiness.

Anyway, *Rocket* and her descendants worked up and down the L. & M. for many years, stopping frequently at Olive Mount Cutting so that the professional engravers could do pictures of them. J. M. W. Turner did the first one and called it 'Rain, Steam and Speed' and although his rather strange impressionist manner didn't show you much of the engine, the rain is unmistakably true to life for it was a very wet district round there: the name RAIN-hill, for example, was not for nothing.

Stephenson surveys Chat Moss.

Before leaving the L. & M. we must mention the loco called *Lion*. He – or she – was, and still is a beauty and now lives in the Paint Shop at Crewe having been built in 1838 by Todd, Kitson & Laird. They took it in turns, Laird left after a while to make Camels so the other two must take the credit for designing the most beautiful funnel in the business. Now as with most things of beauty, nobody thought *Lion* worth keeping after she had got a bit old, but a great service to posterity was rendered by that noble, good, and artistic body known as The Mersey Docks and Harbour Board of blessed and immortal memory, for they took *Lion* and used her as a stationary boiler, needless to say he (or she) did a grand job boiling stationery for they had a lot of paper work, and anyway in Liverpool, you never know which ship the stationery has come from, so to be on the safe side you always boil it.

Talking of vandalism, not that the M.D. & H. Board were that, but just talking of it; did you ever hear the like of the Swindon people who cut up *North Star* and *Lord of the Isles!* Oh, I know they repented and later made a replica of *North Star*, but what a sin to cut up the original! It served them right when, in expiation, they were made to change all their lines one Sunday to 4′ 8½″ gauge.

SINCE starting to write this volume I have been getting nasty letters from people who say that I am biased in favour of the Great Western Railway. Now let it be said here and now that I was born and bred almost on top of another railway which for noise, smoke, and general clatter was second to none; I refer of course to the London and North Western Railway. Pause here for raising of hats and genuflection in the direction of Crewe. There can be no doubt that one railway soon established itself, funnel and dome above all rivals in the mid-nineteenth century.

The Grand Junction Railway and the London & Birmingham were the main constituent companies of the giant to be. The former was the section I knew in my youth. Those fire throwing, black little animals of the Crewe era, tore past my garden end as they rushed their private saloons of grouse-shooting gentry to Scotland, or their waggons of best household nuts to the South.

CREWE: What a world of romance that name calls up: MONKS COPPENHALL. Hey, what did you say? Now I bet you didn't know that did you; well, it was the real name of the place before they decided to call it after Lord

Crewe, who had said that they could not build there unless they named it after him. Now you may well ask why they ever chose Crewe in the first place, the Grand Junction had a perfectly good place at Edge Hill though I believe they had to move out so that someone could fight that battle there. Any how they looked for somewhere suitable to put a really grand junction, and there is no doubt that at Crewe they built the grandest junction that ever caused a railway chaos.

The monks of the abbey of Coppenhall were given good compensation by the way, and their old refectory was made into the tea room on Platform 4. You may still see remains of the Gothic vaulting just above the tea urn and much of the present refreshment was originally made by the monks. One rather awkward brother did however put a curse on the station which had usurped his home and has had considerable effect even to this day. It ran some-

MONKS COPPENHALL

One of the original Crewe porters – a redundant monk from the nearby monastery of Monks Coppenhall.

thing like this, 'Oh master porter what wilt thou do when thou wantest to go to Birminghame but art taken on to Monks Coppenhall.'

This station will appear later in our essay on railway architecture so I shall now take you for a trip round the loco works.

Here we are 'Deviation Entrance'. This always puzzles me but I'm sure there was a very good reason for calling it that if Mr Webb decided to.

Have you got your pass? Oh good, because I can't take you in without it, you might be a spy from Swindon or something, they can't be too careful. Here we are at the

Paint Shop. Lovely smell isn't it! Don't bother about the engines looking so big and near. Look as though you are used to walking near them even if you are scared stiff.

By the way this is 1875 you know, so it's no use looking for any 'Mickys' or 'Jubs'. Here is a '*Compound*'. Now this Class were called 'Teutonics', officially, and we must put you in the picture about this compound business. The name, like so many others, is a corruption of a name which a certain driver called it when he was trying to make it start at Euston. He said 'CONFOUND the engine' as he tried to make both sets of wheels go round the same way. He did add other remarks, but the explosion of the low pressure cylinder luckily drowned them. Anyhow the name stuck and got twisted in the way names do into *Compound*. Funny in a way isn't it!

Francis Webb was the designer of these engines. He was a real martinet, whatever that is, and if you were thinking of working for him and his friend Ramsbottom here at Crewe you had to be careful.

Ah, here is dear old *Cornwall*. Webb didn't build the original which I mentioned earlier, he just made it better and put the boiler in the right place. Here is *Hardwicke* too. These engines will eventually be moved to Clapham

Mr Webb designed a chain brake, which very often did.

One of Mr Webb's ideas, which he abandoned.

so that it will not be so convenient for northern fans to look at them. What matters though for all these northerners are not likely to stay up north much longer as the drift to the south will start in a decade or two.

Now here is the Tender Shop but before we go further let me point out that I don't really count tenders as permanent parts of engines, but if you like I will wait outside while you have a look. By the way, tenders must have at least six wheels to count. Four won't do, and eight is just show off. As I wait for you I will look at these engines standing on the tracks outside. Ah, what names! *Problem*, *Pet*, *Experiment*, *Puzzle* (a compound), *Jamie Jeanes*, *Fury*, *Cerebos*, *Daz*, *Etcetera*. Ah, there's a batch of the great ones!

Oh hello, here you come, out of the Tender Shop. I warned you that there was not much to a tender but at least I must point out that here at Crewe, they make engines from start to finish. They first dig up the iron ore from the Monks Coppenhall mines; then they smelt it in their own steel works; they make their own gas, and even have some left over for the town to have; they turn out engines rather like cars were done later on, except the locomotives last much longer! None of that new-fangled fibre-glass over rust on these. They are strong and simple, no superfluous puffing here, the Webb compounds only puffed twice to each wheel rev, thus saving two lots of puffs compared with the usual. Puff, puff, puff, puff.

This is the boiler shop, there's nothing much to a boiler really, it's just a thing on which to put the funnel and dome, and, of course, the safety valve!

Now there is one very important part of an engine which I must admit I usually skip when I am describing it to a beginner, its the Valve Gear. Some considerate designers put it out of sight and you can just mumble about eccentrics, etc., and mention David Joy and nobody can argue with you, unless they are really prepared to get filthy poking around under the boiler and checking on you. However, there are others like the Russian *Walschaerts* and the Italian film producer, Caprotti, who show all the parts on the outside and make no end of trouble. It's really no use my pretending that I know much about them, so I shall leave it to the experts in that field, but if any of you would like to help me out and can write a full description of a Walschaerts gear, on a post card please, I should be very surprised, but very grateful.

Now to conclude our tour of the great Crewe Works in the Webb era we must pay a visit to the most important place of all – the Engine Naming Studio.

You must be very quiet as we go in because this shop is entirely staffed by poets who have all passed their exams with honours and are very sensitive folk. These exams are oral and Mr Webb sits at his oak desk in a subdued light while he fires questions at the prospective engine name thinker upper.

Crewe: The engine naming studio.

'Who was Cerberus, and how did he differ from the average dog?'

'Who was dipped into the Styx?'

'Complete the following quotation – If this glass doth fall. Farewell then lu – – – – – – – – – ', etc., etc.

They cut all the names while appropriate music is played, Handel for *Samson*, Pythagoras for *Problem* and the croaking chorus for *Eunomia* – Oh I could go on for ages, but if you like I won't.

As we go out of the old works here at Crewe we shall pass the venerable Clock Tower. This was used as a back-drop for all engine photographs in the great days and talking of photographs, they had to be done very secretly in those times because of men.

Yes, men! If you let it be known that you were thinking of posing a locomotive for a picture anywhere, as soon as the man went under his black cloth, a whole swarm of men would clamber all over the engine and strike attitudes. It was rather like those pictures of big game hunters standing with their foot on the neck of some unfortunate lion and I think the men rather liked to lean on the front buffers, or sit on the boiler for the same sort of reason. If you look at one of these pictures you will see that the men usually avoid the tender, it was a bit messy on the coal I suppose, though on some very old tenders there was sometimes a special sort of covered seat for a guard to sit in and look backwards along the train to see if it was still there. Oh it sometimes *wasn't*! Imagine the scene when this sort of first reserve guard had to crawl over the coal and gasp to the driver something like, 'Third composite lav. set on loan Wolvton. Broke away two miles back.' It was no laughing matter, but they later introduced corridor stock and those concertina things held the coaches together. That bit of wobbly floor gave a lot of

Early railway photographers
had a lot of trouble –

– with MEN !

Examining the genuine Gothic above the tea urn.

trouble at first, you know the bit in the concertina part, but eventually it was accepted rather as one goes onto those trick wobbly floors at fair grounds. I must admit that I always jump it in case it catches me with one foot in each coach and the coupling goes.

Well that was Crewe Works that was. Let us now go to the station and have a cup of tea. I can show you that bit of genuine Gothic architecture I mentioned earlier. Besides the next chapter is all about railway architecture.

'– and one for the pot.'

THE ancient Greeks were never called upon to build a railway station, nor were the Gothic builders but the railway architects did it for them. Think of the outworks of St Pancras, or better still, don't. And what about Euston with its Doric propylaea? Of course, it's gone now, but I do hear that the manager of the Parthenon has bought it to do some repairs. The early railways were keen to impress, they were no fools in those days and knew that a good block of buildings was good publicity, although the word hadn't been invented yet.

The original railway gothic was thought up by a Sir John de Beechiman, who lived by the Liverpool & Manchester. He was so keen on Gothic that he made them put gothic cabs on the engines and erect gothic signals.

Look out when you next stop at a station which hasn't been converted into a sort of ice cream parlour by the modernisation boys. Look up at the vaulted roof; look at the stained glass. It certainly is too, let your eyes travel down the cast-iron column cunningly used as down spout to the patterned brickwork – HUDSONS DRY SOAP, STEPHENS INK, GAS METERS, PORTERS ROOM. See the ornamental border of the platform awning – such inventive wood decoration. One often wonders how long the joiner's sanity lasted as he did those repeating saw cuts year in year out. The only place where ornament was lacking was down on the tracks, but modern science has now come to our aid. Here we now have a selection of paper decor – cigarette packets, ice cream wrappers, paper cups, and a real collector's piece – a SHUNT WITH CARE in tasteful Gill Sans.

Am I getting cynical? You must stop me if I do, because I am only too well aware how easy it is to scoff at the Victorian builders and one must be careful because those Victorian things are coming back into fashion. Think of the paintings of Augustus Egg. His 'FIRST CLASS' a fine piece of railway art, and the girl with her dad is nice too. Romantic? Well perhaps, but how about Daumier's 'Troisiemme Classe' (Third Class, to you.)

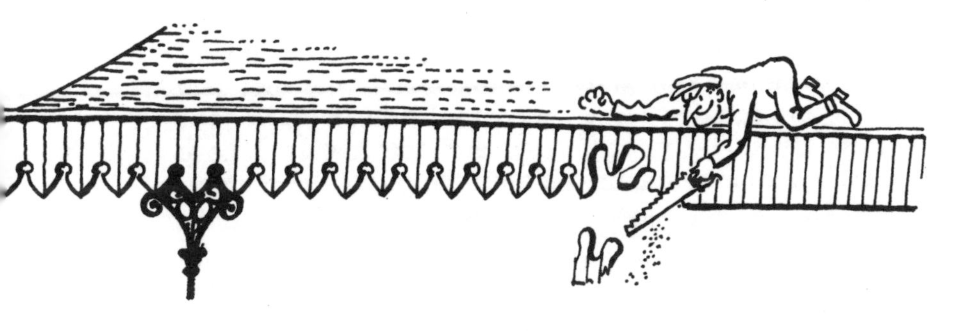

Repeating saw cuts – joiner goes mad.

Trust the French! life in the raw I call it, though it did the railways no good, I can tell you.

Whether I should or not I always count viaducts as architecture. The Ancient Romans had the right idea but they were stuck for something to do with them after they had built them. What use is the Pont du Gard with no trains to go over it? Let me show you my favourite viaduct, it is known locally as Lockspittle Arches and words fail me in praise of this genuine Locke masterpiece. Some will claim that Dragworth bridge is the better but each one to his taste. It's no use me trying to describe it or even to draw it, although I am a very talented artist. You must go and see it for yourself.

Take a single to Lockspittle (Sats exc.) and when you are about half a mile from the Blabworth East Box, pull the cord and jump. Time this well, you will land just short of the viaduct; if you hesitate – well, count three and pull the rip-cord.

Assuming that you *have* timed it right and paid the £5, wait until the train has gone and there it is – grim and mossy, high and horrid, and there, miles below, is Slabbermill Cut. How on earth they ever built these things beats me. Fancy lugging a blooming great voussoir up here. I know they had sort of cranes, but those holes in the stones are nothing to do with that. They are where Oliver Cromwell shot at it.

Voussoirs? Well I did warn you earlier in the book that there were some catching words but I will explain. They are the stones which form the arch on each side of the Key Stone. You know I think that is the first real piece of information I have put into this book up to now. I must try to be more factual and fortunately I have saved the best architecture bit until the end of the chapter.

CONWAY CASTLE was built by the Chester to Holyhead Railway to protect the workmen who were building the Tubular Bridge. They had a lot of trouble from the Welsh who were in league with the Great Western, and the castle was constantly manned by crossbowmen while the navvies put the bridge up.

The Romans built some fine viaducts.

Conway tubular bridge was floated into position thus.

The tube girders had to be floated into place and the first got away, but Stephenson said not to worry, they would probably catch it at Menai and use it up on the other bridge. I don't think anyone will deny that the castle suits the bridge very well. It was an old custom that all engines should whistle as they went through the bridge so that the crossbowmen would know it was a friend coming, and that custom is still observed.

TUNNELS don't really count as architecture but we had better mention a few so as not to hurt anyone's feelings. *Box*, *Woodhead* (*old*), *Kilsby*, *Blea Moore* (I'm not sure if that is a tunnel or a viaduct, but let's leave it in).

Oh goodness, I forgot Saltash Bridge, forgive me, G.W.R. fans, this really is a masterpiece of Victorian art, yes *art*. I maintain that the real artists of that age were the engineers. Pity they didn't think of closing the railway

Very early photograph of interior of Box Tunnel— or perhaps Woodhead, we forget exactly which.

Mr Brunel deciding to build a tunnel at Box.

over it sooner and saving all that money they have spent on the road bridge.

Oh dear, I keep thinking of things to add on, just like Gilbert Scott did to St Pancras. How about the dear little Gothic country stations.

I really must pay homage to them. How about a poem?

Oh Wellow, Wellow, down the line.
And Blandford Forum too,
Dear Evercreech is out of reach,
Now 'The Pines' does not pass through.

Will Bournemouth West go with the rest,
Now that the S and D,
Has heard its last "West Country" blast?
Ask Beeching, don't ask me!

WE have gone a long way since we started and yet we haven't mentioned signals. We have been very lucky not to nave had a crash if you ask me, however you can relax now because I am going to clarify the whole position.

Early rail travel was a lighthearted matter and it took time for it to become the serious, sad, affair which it now is. You got up steam; fastened the waggons on behind, and off you went spinning down to Darlington! This was fine as long as you only had one engine, but when you had saved up enough to buy another, then the trouble began. You needed control of traffic. Yes, you've guessed it. The Police stepped in. Well, you know how good they are at moving things on. They have a sort of grudge about anything stationary, so they were just the men for the job.

Anyway business was rather slack for them just then, the last sheep stealer had been hanged and Jack the Ripper hadn't happened yet, so what better than to give the Bobby a flag and tell him to keep an eye on things.

Yes, the first signal was a flag, but they soon wanted

more than one, as people do and eventually they had one for almost everything: STOP, GO, SOMEONE WANTS TO OVERTAKE and OIL ON THE ROAD. You know the kind of thing. Well, the name 'Bobby' has stuck and you will hear the older railwaymen refer to the signalman as such. I like these old customs, there are many about, like saying 'on the down' or 'on the up'. To the uninitiated this can be confusing when, for instance, you discover that as you are belting *down* Shap, you are really on the *up*. Get out your atlas if you like and work it out.

After the bobby got tired they had balls on poles and discs which spun around, but when you read that I. K. Brunel used to get an engine out and go off on the *wrong line* to look for *Ajax* when it was late, it makes you wonder if they took signals seriously.

The semaphore signal was the final idea. They hadn't thought about those traffic lights with too many ambers yet, and as might be expected, the L.N.W.R. made the best ones, unless, that is, you are a G.W. fan.

Those tall signals were almost sculpture, in fact they were a lot better than some I know: they had personality! I well remember a lovely 60-footer near to our garden which I fell in love with.

When the Railway Mania really took on epidemic proportions it was not just a case of a line here and another parallel to it. Oh no! there were lines crossing and going under and over until the poor bobby (signalman remember) was fair mazed. As usual in our Island story, the hour produced the man. Saxby, thought out a system of interlocking and by jove it was foolproof, unless some fool of a driver didn't obey a signal.

Interlocking is a simple system by which the signalman has to do something before he can do something else and if he doesn't he can't.

The L.N.W.R. were best at signal boxes, they built the

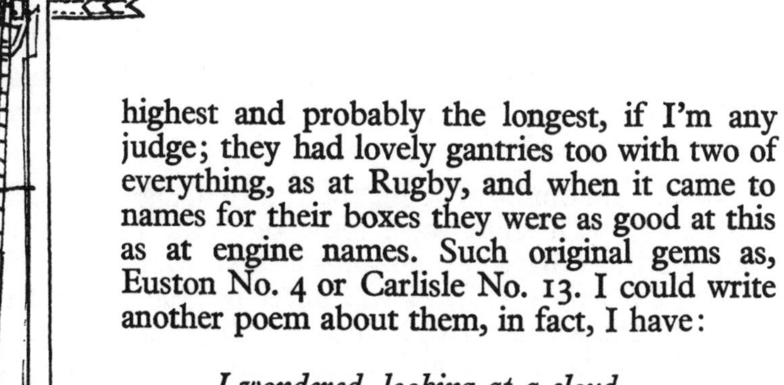

highest and probably the longest, if I'm any judge; they had lovely gantries too with two of everything, as at Rugby, and when it came to names for their boxes they were as good at this as at engine names. Such original gems as, Euston No. 4 or Carlisle No. 13. I could write another poem about them, in fact, I have:

I wondered, looking at a cloud
Of steam escaping from the gills
Of 594, *a* 4-4-0,
If drivers still gave tallow pills.
Beside the line like stately trees
The semaphores drooped in the breeze.
The wires beside me danced, but see,
The milk train's here, its half past three.
And oft when on my couch I think,
Of reminiscent railway lore.
Before my inward eyes they wink.
The dear departed semaphore.

I must admit that the foregoing epic is not entirely my own. The original was written by a gentleman who lived not very far from Shap, and often spotted. He actually wrote that poem on Westminster Bridge after coming down on the 'Lakes'.

Now I am doubtful about the future of signalling. One could toy with short-wave radio or Asdic but you can never tell, perhaps the police will take over again. You know, I bet they do, they will never be able to stand the sight of those blue electric jobs standing on the spur at Crewe for hours wasting good watts and causing an obstruction.

WHEN the Prince Regent made the South Coast popular with his goings on at Brighton, he unwittingly helped in the production of Gladstone. Unless you are well informed on railway matters, you may well misunderstand the significance of this. Gladstone was a Prime Minister, we know but to all railway addicts the name only means an 0-4-2.

The L.B.S.C.R. came later than Prinny, but the following of Bucks and Blades which he attracted got together and founded a private line to transport them to their orgies in the caves of the South Downs. The club they formed was called, if you will pardon the expression, the Hellfire Club. Now it was rather a naughty club but we are not going to dwell on that, plenty of other books do that these days! No, at great sacrifice we will stick to the railway side of it. Now about these Club Trains. The line ran from Regency Station, later called Victoria, when she came; to the Pavilion terminus in Brighton, but there was a secret branch to the H.F. caves which left the main line at Clapham Junction where nobody noticed it go.

Brighton has still a certain flavour of the period about it and the week-end traffic on the line always was heavy. In the early days you could get a plaguey great dish of sack or scull cocktail in the Gazebo Cars which the line had built to match the Pavilion at Brighton. The Devil worshippers had a special branch built to his Dyke, but the climb was a little too much for the 'terriers' and they abandoned it.

The electric line to London came later, after they had tried it out between the pier and Black Rock, but that's another story.

How well I remember the yellow beauty of those

Special Gazebo car built by the LB & SCR for use on the Hellfire Club Specials.

L.B.S.C. engines with their rattling six-wheelers as they tore through Hassocks or Preston Park full of pleasure-bent populace and lady friends. It has not changed much and you can see the line for yourself if you like, by buying a ticket so I will not burden you with my personal memories.

THE CHESHIRE LINES COMMITTEE

Now as the L.B.S.C. was born of the renegade Regency, the C.L.C. was different. It was never born really. It just crept unnoticed over the Cheshire fields, much as it has been doing ever since.

Chester is its southern terminus, and of course you all know what that means: Romans. The thermae of Trajan are the model for the C.L.C. terminus there, and the tepidarium is the tea room; the frigidarium is the waiting room. The C.L.C. never owned a single engine. Yes, it's true. They built lines, and waggons, but they drew the line at locomotives. The farmers in that green and pleasant

The C.L.C. had no locomotives.

dairy county were the opponents of the locomotive, they said that the cows wouldn't like it. Of course the cows were behind it all, you will remember how we discussed the feud which grew up between them and the early railways. Cheshire cows are very influential and they made it so difficult for the C.L.C. by getting on the line, and chewing signal wires, that in the end the directors promised not to build any engines.

On the other hand, the Midland, Great Central and Great Northern didn't care what cows thought, and they sent their engines into Cheshire and almost succeeded in providing a good train service there.

Salt mines or salt cellars, as the smaller ones are called, occur in Mid Cheshire. The Romans left a lot of the stuff after paying their soldiers' salaries in it, and the mines are still a source of danger to the railway as subsidences frequently occur, often quite unexpectedly, and if you are waiting for a train any time, you should be prepared for it to be very late, or even not to appear at all as it has quite probably dropped into a salt mine or something. The mineral traffic on this line is very heavy and a lump of Derbyshire limestone counts as equal to three civilians.

But no, I must not be nasty, it's a grand little line, I have seen no railway in the length and breadth of the land to compare with it and by the way, be honest, did you know there WAS such a railway? You didn't? Well, see what I mean? Those cows have used their influence to keep it out of the news, but I had better shut up about it because it has just dawned on me that Dr Beeching never mentioned it in his plan. Perhaps he hasn't heard of it either!

POST SCRIPTUM

Of course, the L.N.W.R. was the railway of most distinction and even went to the length of painting one of Mr. Webb's 2-2-2-2 Compounds (actually 2054 *Queen Empress*) in white livery for H.M.'s diamond jubilee.

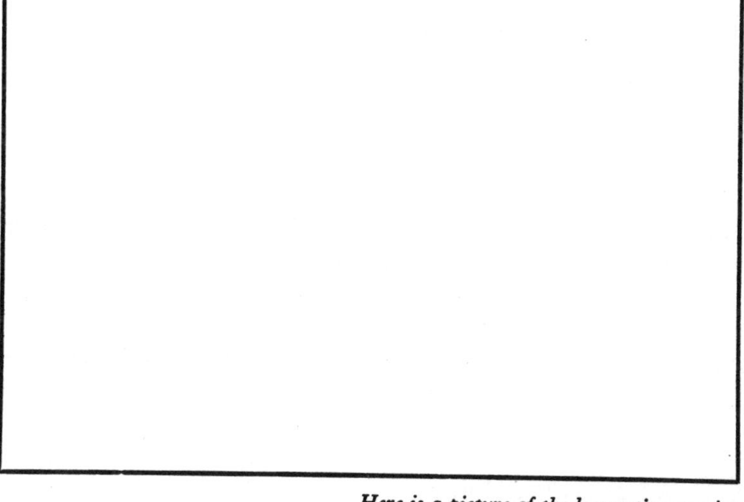

Here is a picture of the locomotive running light down Shap in a rather heavy Scotch (-or rather, north west English) mist.

You will agree with me I am sure that railways neatly divide themselves for historical purposes into clear-cut sections – 'The L.N.W.R.' and 'the Rest', form the main headings, but if you are a G.W.R. fan of course then you can substitute their initials. Let us look at a few of the other things, other than locomotives, you know, things like chocolate machines and weigh-bridges.

STATION SEATS

Now here we can really see the poetry of the designer at its most sedate. You don't want to make a seat look speedy, you want an inviting sort of cast-iron rustic couch, with cast-iron logs for arms and legs and a back with the station name in raised letters which become embossed into the flesh of the tired traveller.

I am always sorry that Conan Doyle never thought of that as a Sherlock Holmes' clue. Something like this:

'I see that you came by way of Llandudno Junction, my

dear Watson,' remarked Holmes as he executed the 'devil's trill' on his violin.

'How on earth did you know *that* Holmes? I purposely came to Baker Street that way to throw Moriarty off the scent.'

'Elementary my dear Watson, as you took off your vest to change for dinner I saw the letters UDNALL embossed on your latissimus dorsi.'

We could include here the old one about WET PAINT but perhaps you've heard it.

There is no doubt that the most comfortable station seat

is a mail bag on a truck; the seats themselves are not designed for comfort but to enhance the beauty of the station.

COAL YARD SIGNS

'Coal Jones Merchant' is quite acceptable, here, but I must stick to the unusual and try to convey the meaning of just one I know which says, '. . . EXORS of S.

GRIMEWORTH, FUEL SPECIALISTS.' Now let us break it down,

(*a*) Exors. Well, you know how they get rid of ghosts. I think that this has something to do with that.

(*b*) Fuel specialists. I am getting a picture here of the white-coated expert, with stethoscope to ears, listening to a lump of coal and murmuring something to himself which you are not supposed to hear. He will probably charge the earth for his services – but coal merchants themselves do anyway, don't they!

PASSENGERS MUST CROSS THE LINE BY THE OVERBRIDGE

They have been trying ever since that unhappy affair with Husskison on the L. & M., to convince passengers that *only porters know how to cross a line without dire consequences.* Crossing a busy road is child's play compared with crossing the line when the timetable tells you clearly enough that the next train is at 4.45, and even then on Saturdays only and today is not Saturday. However, there it is, and you might as well obey it. If it is a third-rail electric then I advise you to use that bridge, although there's only 600 odd volts waiting to snap at your ankles.

FIRE BUCKETS

Engines throw fire. The L.N.W.R. was, as with most other things, best at this too, somehow they never managed to burn down Dudley Port, which would have made a spectacular blaze, however, those red fire buckets hanging round the corner by the 'what's its', stand ready for any

emergency. In case of fire, you unhook, and throw the litter inside onto the flames to make it worthwhile to call the Fire Service. Railways have not yet, of course, discovered the fire extinguisher.

LAMP ROOMS

I must confess that I am doubtful about these. What really goes on behind those paint blistered doors? Lamps they tell us! But I fear that they are just a front for much more unpleasant business. My theory is that they are padded cells where they put the poor drivers who have lost their reason and started driving trains from the wrong end.

TIME TABLES

You may wonder why I put these in the oddments' section like this. Well, I feel that you should know the truth. There are two time-tables. Yes, two! One is the one

they let the likes of you and me see. The other is the REAL one which is for drivers only, and must not be divulged to the public. It is reverently called the 'Service Book'.

You may have been standing fuming for ages on a station waiting for the train which the time-table said was due half an hour ago, but you haven't seen the WORKING time-table. What is probably happening is that the driver is hiding behind the corner with his train because he has just consulted his secret time-table and found he has half an hour to spare. This is called 'recovery time'.

PLACE PENNY IN SLOT MACHINES

Most of these have now been snapped up by the Victoria and Albert, but you might come across one on some forgotten halt. If you do, and you put a penny in the slot, *and* you get a piece of chocolate. Please don't eat it! It is at least 30 years old.

EPIGRAMS CHALKED ON WAGGONS

These are the last remaining creative outlet for the poor displaced poets who became redundant when the Engine Naming Studio was closed at Crewe. You may while away many a tedious half hour if your train happens to be held up opposite a goods yard, by trying to decipher the chalked epigrams, pictograms and anagrams on the waggon sides. I wish you luck but the only one I have ever managed was one which said, EMT GARS YD TUSDY. Try it and see.

NOT IN COMMON USE

These waggons and Guards Vans are the élite of the force. They are for the use of the higher class guards who don't find it easy to mix with the rabble. The interiors are furnished in the best of taste – Sheraton grub cupboard, and Adam coke stove. The brake wheel is of filigree work and the guard wears gloves to avoid soiling his hands. I don't hold with 'em myself. Why can't all vans be IN common use, that's what I want to know!

ON LOAN TO . . .

The railways are very jealous of their property. They keep it very much to themselves and if they ever lend another depot anything like an old 6-wheeler from the E.D. with tools and first-aid kit; then they make sure that the borrowers never forget where it came from, by painting ON LOAN, etc., on the frame.

The borrowers are rather unfair about it and never send it back. I can vouch for one such six-wheeler having stood in the yard siding for 12 years at a station which must be nameless.

THE LICKEY INCLINE

This is an oddment in that it is unique. It has had more than its fair share of trespassers with cameras in its long history. Shap perhaps comes second, but Lickey is tops as far as the business of showing trains out of the horizontal – or perpendicular, for that matter – goes.

Early days on the Lickey.

Racing to the North – a popular sport before the invention of the motor car.

It was built so that engines could show off. There is not much drama in going steadily along on the flat and when they found a hill not quite big enough to tunnel or cut, then they put an incline and dared the loco designers to build something strong enough to climb it alone. LICKEY won, and still reigns supreme unless those blessed diesels have done it alone, but I'm not going to count that. I don't like diesels.

THE LAST ODDMENT WE WILL MENTION IS THE . . . RAILWAY MANIAC!

Age does not enter into this. You can have 'em 8 or 80 – and you do! I am between those ages I will confide and so is my Publisher. Your true maniac can spot a missing or a supernumerary nut or washer on a locomotive, he can

Where stations are closed, the old mailbag pick-up could be adapted.

get angry about any slight on his favourite company, and tell you shed numbers and head codes even though they are quite useless. Do I see some railway maniac reader going white with anger? Well, see what I mean?

Least said soonest mended, so let's press on to the final chapter where I hope to tie up all the loose ends.

Summary and Glossary

ALAS it is almost time to ring down the curtain on this pageant of railway history. Not that I think that railways have finished performing, but they have passed out of the period when they interest me, I'm afraid. Railways without steam are not railways for me. The future may bring hover trains hurtling waggons full of best atoms across the map, but for me the steam engine is a *must*, as far as railways are concerned.

I do not think I have missed anything out in this very thorough survey of the railways history have I?

Carriages? Well, the very name tells you that there has been so little development there that it need not concern

us. After all the coach in which the noble Lord of the manor progressed across Britain in the early nineteenth century was the model for all later railway coaches. There were more wheels added but the interiors were identical and the riding has not improved.

The track? Here again the thing is easily cleared up. Take two fish plates. Two bulls' heads. One flat bottom, and add a packet of expansion gaps and that is it.

Finally let us put all the remaining items into an alphabetical appendix, thusly –

A AXEL BOX, see journal. Used for stopping trains when brakes fail to do so. It gets hot and stop you must!

B BLACKPOOL. The Mecca of all Excursions.

C CYLINDER. This is where steam oozed in and pushed the piston back, remember?

D DYNOMITING CAR. This is a special coach which has all sorts of gadgets inside for seeing if the engine is any good.

E ENGINEER'S SALOON. Here we have the ultimate in comfort and posh coachwork. The engineer and his hangers on, get a special engine, and go for spins when the monotony of office work gets too much. The cuisine is excellent.

F FLANGES. Without some of these the train would not stay on the line; so I should always go and look if your engine has got a good set.

G GREAT WESTERN. Not to be confused with Great Eastern which was a ship as well as a railway, and there was a ship called Great Western too, so extra care is necessary!

H HORSE BOX is the name given to the covered van which houses a groom and a horse. You will remember that we mentioned cows as being rude to trains. Well, horses never were, and so the railways treat them well. Actually eight horses are regarded as equal to forty men.

I INJECTOR. This is the way they get the water into the boiler against pressure. I can't understand it myself but it seems to work.

J JUBILEE. These were a class of engine which I very much admired because they roared instead of puffing.

K KIDSGROVE. This is the station either at the bottom of the Lickey Incline or at the top, I can never remember which.

L Well this is easy. Lickey Incline near to Kidsgrove... or is it Bromsgrove?

M MOTOR TRAIN. These were called 'push and pull' later. They were an optical illusion really. The man at the wrong end was just a decoy. The real driver kept out of sight behind the cab sides.

N NUMBERING. Oh, now for it. This superfluous practice was invented by a certain Mr Allan who was a numismological wizard – and a GREAT BENEFACTOR.

O OIL CORK. These are those primitive old bottle corks which they stick over big-end bearings and they then fall out. After all the directors' dinners they go round collecting the corks, so they are never short!

P PRECURSOR. These engines were built at Crewe at two different periods. Webb built some small 2-4-0s called that, and Whale produced the later ones of which *Sirocco* was the last to survive. She kept well out of the way at Llandudno Junction until somebody split on her.

Q QUEER-LOOKING ENGINES. How about the Kitson Still?

R RUNNING COSTS. Ask any railwayman how much it costs to run that train you go to work on, and you will wonder if the wheels are platinum or uranium.

S STEAM. This is being rudely cast aside in favour of oil, which is a dirty trick, unless you have some oil shares.

T TUBE RAILWAYS. I don't count these myself.

U UNDERGROUND. Much the same but rather like calling radio, wireless.

V VALVE GEAR. Cor blimey, is it this again? Well, there are too many snags here for me to clear up so look at a drawing.

W WATER COLUMN. I'll never forget the day when I saw that diesel driver start to fill up . . .

X XERXES! I'm sure there *must* have been a Crewe engine named that.

Y YORK MUSEUM. Oh, I could write a sonnet, but I won't.

Z That's got him. ZULU, a Gooch engine of the *Lord of the Isles* class.

And ZAMIEL, A 2-4-0 Allan Crewe Goods Number 11.

THE END